9-5-79

The Easy Book of
NUMBERS and NUMERALS

0	1	2	3	4
5	6	7	8	9

The Easy Book of
NUMBERS and NUMERALS

—by David C. Whitney—

—illustrations by Anne Marie Jauss—

FRANKLIN WATTS, INC. | NEW YORK | 1973

ALSO BY THE AUTHOR

The Easy Book of Division
The Easy Book of Fractions
The Easy Book of Multiplication
The Easy Book of Sets
Let's Find Out about Addition
Let's Find Out about Subtraction

Library of Congress Cataloging in Publication Data

Whitney, David C
    The easy book of numbers and numerals.

    SUMMARY: Explains the origin of numerals and
their use in different numbering systems.
    1. Numeration—Juvenile literature. 2. Numerals—
Juvenile literature. [1. Number systems. 2. Numerals]
I. Jauss, Anne Marie, illus. II. Title.
QA141.3.W45   513'.5   73-6695
ISBN 0-531-02597-7

            2 3 4 5 6 7 8 9

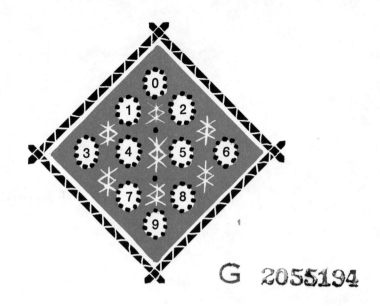

The Easy Book of
NUMBERS and NUMERALS

How many fingers are on this hand?
The answer is *five.*
Five is a NUMBER.

Find the number of cats and the number of
   dogs in the picture.
You can see that the number of dogs is *six.*
   The number of cats is *three.*
A NUMBER is a word that describes *how many*
   there are of something, just as the word
   red describes the color of a fire engine.

Where is the horse in this parade?
The answer also is a number.
You can see that the zebra is *first*.
The camel is *second*. The horse is *third*.

Where in the line is the boy with
the baseball bat?
By counting the numbers *first, second,
third, fourth,* and so on, you see
that the boy is in *fourth* place.

NUMBERS tell *how many* there are of something
or *where something is in a line or series.*
How many people are standing in line at the movie?
The number of people is *six.*
Where in line is the woman with flowers on her hat?
Her number in line is *third.*

To write numbers, you use marks or symbols
   called NUMERALS.
Many, many years ago cavemen understood the
   use of numbers. They used numbers to count
   how many animals they killed when hunting.
The first NUMERALS were the marks that
   the cavemen made to keep track of
   how many animals they had killed.

The caveman had only one NUMERAL—
    a mark that stood for the number *one*.
To keep track of bigger numbers, he had to
    repeat the same mark (NUMERAL)
    for each thing he counted.
To keep count of three animals, he made
    three marks.

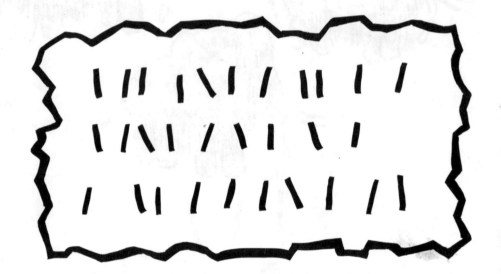

With only one numeral, it is hard to
write or read large numbers.
You have to count each mark to tell
that the numerals on this page
stand for the number *thirty*.

After many years went by, people learned to make
  numerals for larger numbers easier to read.
They began separating the marks into groups of
  five. Then they could count by groups of five.
So, the numerals on this page can be read—
  five, ten, fifteen, twenty, twenty-five, thirty—
  a total of *thirty*.

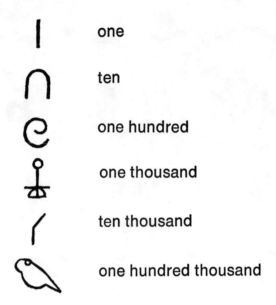

	one
	ten
	one hundred
	one thousand
	ten thousand
	one hundred thousand

About five thousand years ago, the Egyptians began to use different marks or numerals to stand for larger numbers.

They continued to use a single mark for the number one. But they added a picture of an arch to stand for the number ten, a coiled rope for the number one hundred, a lotus for one thousand, a finger for ten thousand, and a tadpole for one hundred thousand.

∩∩ III

Can you tell what number these Egyptian
   numerals stand for?
The order of the numerals does not matter.
   You just add the numerals together to
   get the total number.
There are two tens and three ones. Add
   these together—10 + 10 + 1 + 1 + 1.
You find that the numerals stand for the
   number twenty-three.

About the same time that the Egyptians wrote
   picture numerals, people who lived near
   the eastern end of the Mediterranean Sea
   made numerals with wedge-shaped triangles.
A large triangle turned on its point stood for
   sixty. An arrowhead pointing left stood for ten.
   A small triangle standing on its point was one.
The numerals above are 60 + 10 + 1 + 1 + 1.
   So these numerals stand for the number
   seventy-three.

α	one	ς	six
β	two	ζ	seven
γ	three	η	eight
δ	four	θ	nine
ϵ	five	ι	ten

About 2,500 years ago the Greeks began to use
 the letters of their alphabet as numerals.
The system was hard to read because both words
 and numbers used the same symbols.
In addition to the numerals above, the Greeks
 used other letters to stand for larger numbers.

I one	C one hundred
V five	D five hundred
X ten	M one thousand
L fifty	

After the Greeks, the Romans developed
a system of numerals that used fewer
letters to stand for numbers.
The Roman numerals XXVIII can be read
10 + 10 + 5 + 1 + 1 + 1.
So XXVIII stands for the number
twenty-eight.

Have you noticed that all the numerals you have
seen so far are alike in one important way?
Each of these numeral systems depends on adding
up each of the numerals to find a total number.
They also are alike in another important way.
None has a numeral that stands for *zero.*

||||
||

𒐗𒈦

⚕CПI

βθηζ

XXVIII

More than a thousand years after the Romans developed their numeral system, the Arabs invented a numeral system that used *zero.*

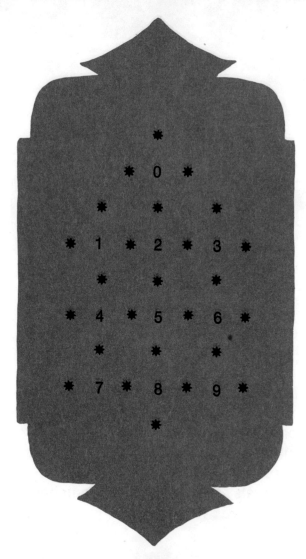

The invention of *zero* made possible the system
of numerals that most people use today.
This system uses ten numerals, as shown above.
Because *decimal* means *ten,* this system of ten
numerals is called the DECIMAL SYSTEM.

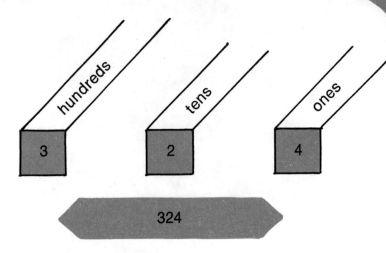

In the decimal system, each numeral has a
    different VALUE, depending on its position
    in a complete number.
In the position farthest to the right, a
    numeral stands for ones. In the next position,
    each numeral stands for tens. In the third
    position, each numeral stands for hundreds.
    And so on.
The numerals above stand for the number
    three hundred twenty-four.

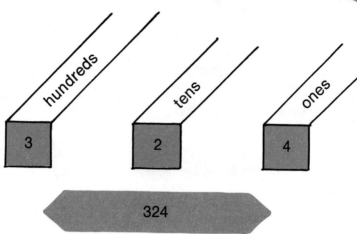

hundreds 3 **tens** 2 **ones** 4

324

In the decimal system, each place has a
value that is ten times larger than
the place to its right.

The number above could be written this way:

$3 \times 10 \times 10 = 300$

$2 \times 10 \times 1 \ = \ 20$

$4 \times 1 \qquad = \ \underline{\quad 4}$

$\qquad\qquad\qquad\quad 324$

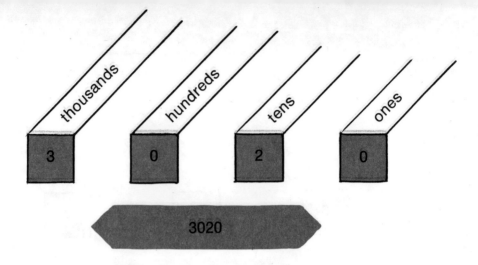

The decimal system could not be developed until the zero was invented. The zero is needed as a PLACE HOLDER in numbers that do not need a numeral for a certain value.

For example, in the number above, there are no hundreds and no ones. The number is read as three thousand twenty.

Using the decimal system, it takes only four numerals to write the number. A caveman would have had to use an entire wall to write such a number, making a total of 3,020 separate marks as numerals.

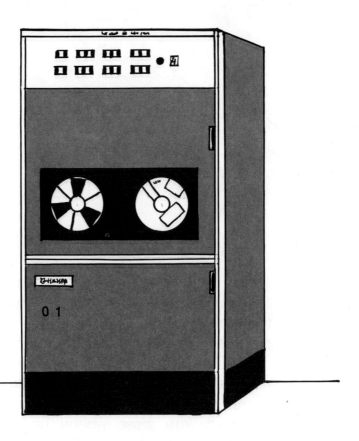

Other numeral systems can be based with more
   or fewer numerals than ten.
Computers use what is called the BINARY SYSTEM
   of numerals. *Binary* means *two.* So the binary
   system uses just two numerals—0 and 1.
In a computer, the 0 is an open switch with
   the electricity turned off. The 1 is a closed
   switch with the electricity turned on. A
   computer can work with numbers more rapidly
   than a person as its switches open and close.

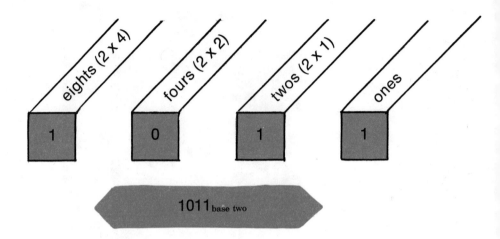

In the binary system, each place has a value two times as large as the place to its right.
In the position farthest to the right, a numeral stands for ones. In the second place, a numeral stands for twos. In the third place, a numeral stands for fours. And so on.
You should write "base two" at the lower right of a binary number to show that it is NOT a decimal number.

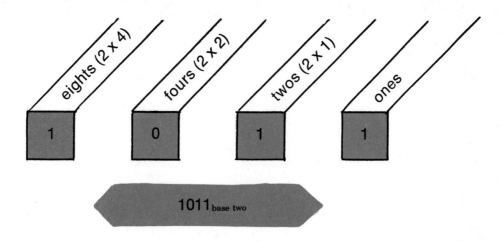

$1011_{\text{base two}}$

The numerals $1011_{\text{base two}}$ stand for
    the decimal number 11.
Here is how you can figure out this
    binary number:

$$1 \times 1 = 1$$
$$1 \times 2 = 2$$
$$0 \times 4 = 0$$
$$1 \times 8 = 8$$
$$1011_{\text{base two}} = \overline{11}$$

You just multiply each numeral by its
    place value and add the results.

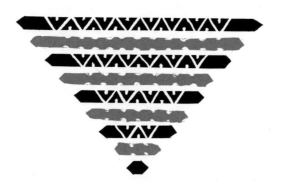

Here are nine binary system problems to work. Use a separate sheet of paper to figure out the decimal number for each of these binary numbers. Then check your answers with the correct answers at the bottom of the page.

1. $101_{\text{base two}}$ 2. $1101_{\text{base two}}$ 3. $10_{\text{base two}}$
4. $111_{\text{base two}}$ 5. $110_{\text{base two}}$ 6. $1001_{\text{base two}}$
7. $11_{\text{base two}}$ 8. $1000_{\text{base two}}$ 9. $100_{\text{base two}}$

ANSWERS:

1. 5   2. 13   3. 2
4. 7   5. 6   6. 9
7. 3   8. 8   9. 4

$$15 = \underline{\quad?\quad}_{\text{base two}}$$

Now you know how to change a base two number into a decimal number. But how do you change a decimal number into a base two number?

Suppose you want to change the decimal number 15 into a base two number.

First, make a table of each of the place values for a base two number, like the table below.

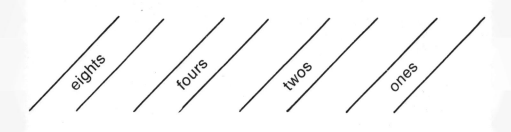

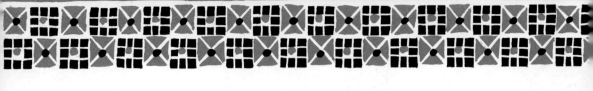

$$15 = ?_{\text{base two}}$$

In changing 15 into a base two number, decide which is the largest base two place value that can be subtracted from 15. 1? 2? 4? 8? 16? The largest that can be subtracted is 8. 15 − 8 = 7. Place a 1 in the eights place of the base two number:

<u>1</u> __ __ __ $_{\text{base two}}$

Next, after the eight has been subtracted, look at the remainder, which is 7. Can the next largest base two place value (4) be subtracted from 7? Yes. 7 − 4 = 3. So, put a 1 in the fours place.

<u>1</u> <u>1</u> __ __ $_{\text{base two}}$

Again, you can subtract the next highest place value (2) from the remainder (3). 3 − 2 = 1. So place a 1 in the twos place.

<u>1</u> <u>1</u> <u>1</u> __ $_{\text{base two}}$

Finally, the last remainder (1) tells you to put a 1 in the ones place.

<u>1</u> <u>1</u> <u>1</u> <u>1</u> $_{\text{base two}}$

So, we see that decimal number 15 equals $1111_{\text{base two}}$.

$$
\begin{aligned}
1 \times 1 &= 1 \\
1 \times 2 &= 2 \\
1 \times 4 &= 4 \\
1 \times 8 &= \underline{8} \\
&\,15
\end{aligned}
$$

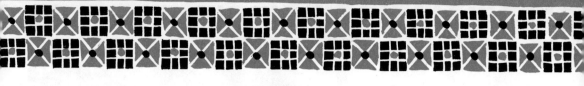

Here are nine problems to work. Figure out the base two
number that is equal to each of these decimal numbers.
Use a separate sheet of paper. Then check your
answers with the correct answers at the bottom of the
page.

1. 3   2. 5   3. 7
4. 2   5. 4   6. 6
7. 8   8. 10   9. 12

0 1 2 3 4

Other numeral systems are based on other sets of
   numerals.
Quinary means *five.* So the QUINARY SYSTEM is based
   on five numerals—0, 1, 2, 3, 4.

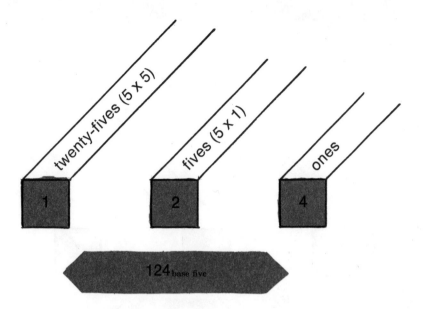

In the quinary system, each place value is five times as
   great as the place value to its right.
In the position farthest to the right, a numeral stands for
   ones. In the second position, a numeral stands for fives.
   In the third place, it stands for twenty-fives. And so on.
You should write "base five" to the lower right of a quinary
   number to show that it is NOT a decimal number.

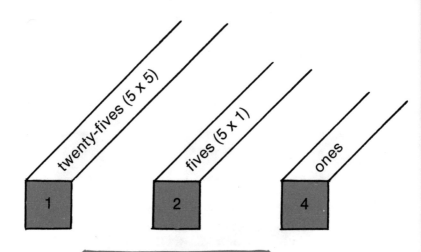

124~base five~ = 39

The quinary number $124_{\text{base five}}$ is equal to the decimal number 39. Here is how to figure out why.

Multiply each numeral in the quinary number by its place value. Then add. The answer is the decimal number that is equal to the quinary number.

So, to change $124_{\text{base five}}$ into a decimal number:

$$1 \times 25 = 25$$
$$2 \times 5 = 10$$
$$4 \times 1 = \underline{4}$$
$$124_{\text{base five}} = 39$$

$98 = \underline{\ ?\ }_{\text{base five}}$

How do you change the decimal number 98 into a base five number?

First, make a table of each of the place values for a base five number, like the table below.

twenty-fives

fives

ones

_____   _____   _____

$$98 = \underline{\ ?\ }_{\text{base five}}$$

In changing 98 into a base five number, decide which is the largest base five place value that can be divided into 98. 1? 5? 25?

The largest that can be used to divide into 98 is 25.

$$\begin{array}{r} 3 \\ 25\,/\,\overline{98} \\ 75 \\ \hline 23 \end{array}$$

Because 25 divided into 98 gives you 3, this tells you to put a 3 in the twenty-fives place.

$$\underline{3}\quad\underline{\ }\quad\underline{\ }\quad{}_{\text{base five}}$$

After the 98 has been divided, look at the remainder, which is 23. Can the next largest base five place value (5) be divided into 23? Yes.

$$\begin{array}{r} 4 \\ 5\,/\,\overline{23} \\ 20 \\ \hline 3 \end{array}$$

Because 5 divided into 23 gives you 4, this tells you to put a 4 in the fives place.

$$\underline{3}\quad\underline{4}\quad\underline{\ }\quad{}_{\text{base five}}$$

In the final step, you see there are 3 ones in the remainder, so you know a 3 should be put in the ones place.

$$\underline{3}\quad\underline{4}\quad\underline{3}\quad{}_{\text{base five}}$$

So, we see the decimal number 98 equals $343_{\text{base five}}$.

Here are twelve quinary system problems to work. Figure out your answers on a separate sheet of paper. Then check your answers with the correct answers at the bottom of the page.

Change these base five numbers into decimal numbers:
1. $4_{\text{base five}}$ 2. $11_{\text{base five}}$ 3. $34_{\text{base five}}$
4. $111_{\text{base five}}$ 5. $32_{\text{base five}}$ 6. $121_{\text{base five}}$

Change these decimal numbers into base five numbers:
7. 5 8. 9 9. 15
10. 31 11. 48 12. 63

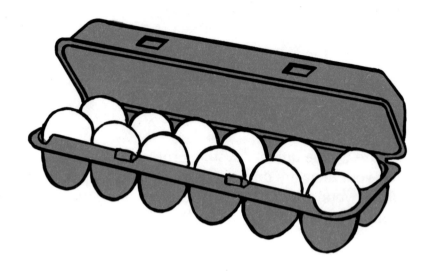

You have learned to use numeral systems with two
numerals (binary), five numerals (quinary), and ten
numerals (decimal). But you also can use numeral
systems with *more* than ten numerals.

People often count objects by the dozen. For example,
twelve eggs make a dozen. A dozen dozen, or 144,
are called a *gross.*

Duodecimal means *twelve.* So a system based on twelve
numerals is called a DUODECIMAL SYSTEM. The
twelve numerals used in the duodecimal system are
0, 1, 2, 3, 4, 5, 6, 7, 8, 9, T for ten, and E for eleven.

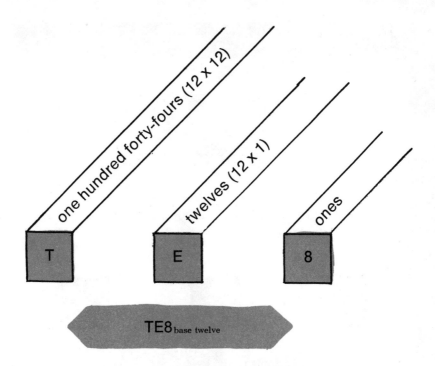

In the duodecimal system, each place value in a number is twelve times as great as the place to its right.

In the position farthest to the right, a numeral stands for ones. In the second place, a numeral stands for twelves. In the third place, the value is for one hundred forty-fours. And so on.

You should write "base twelve" to the lower right of a duodecimal number to show it is NOT a decimal number.

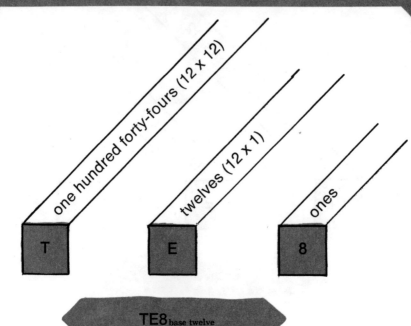

The duodecimal number TE8$_\text{base twelve}$ is equal to the decimal number 1,580. Here is how to figure out why.
Multiply each numeral in the duodecimal number by its place value. Then add. The answer is the decimal number that is equal to the duodecimal number.
So, to change TE8$_\text{base twelve}$ into a decimal number:

$$
\begin{aligned}
\text{T (10)} \times 144 &= 1{,}440 \\
\text{E (11)} \times\ \ 12 &=\ \ \ 132 \\
8\ \ \ \ \times\ \ \ \ 1 &=\ \ \ \ \ \ 8 \\
\hline
\text{TE8}_\text{base twelve}\ \ &= \overline{1{,}580}
\end{aligned}
$$

$$254 = \underline{?}_{\text{base twelve}}$$

How do you change the decimal number 254 into a base twelve number?

First, make a table of each of the place values for a base twelve number, like the table below.

one hundred forty-fours   twelves   ones

_____   _____   _____

In changing 254 into a base twelve number, decide which is the largest base twelve place value that can be divided into 254. 1? 12? 144?

The largest that can be used to divide into 254 is 144.

$$
\begin{array}{r}
1 \\
144 \, / \, \overline{254} \\
144 \\
\hline
110
\end{array}
$$

Because 144 divided into 254 gives you 1, this tells you to put a 1 in the one hundred forty-fours place:

$$\underline{1} \quad \underline{} \quad \underline{} \quad _{\text{base twelve}}$$

After the 144 has been divided, look at the remainder, which is 110. Can the next largest base twelve place value (12) be divided into 110? Yes.

$$
\begin{array}{r}
9 \\
12 \, / \, \overline{110} \\
108 \\
\hline
2
\end{array}
$$

Because 12 divided into 110 gives you 9, this tells you to put a 9 in the twelves place:

$$\underline{1} \quad \underline{9} \quad \underline{} \quad _{\text{base twelve}}$$

In the final step, you see there are 2 ones in the remainder, so you know a 2 should be put in the ones place.

$$\underline{1} \quad \underline{9} \quad \underline{2} \quad _{\text{base twelve}}$$

So, we see the decimal number 254 equals $192_{\text{base twelve}}$.

Here are twelve duodecimal system problems to work.
  Figure out your answers on a separate sheet of paper.
  Then check your answers with the correct answers
  at the bottom of the page.

Change these base twelve numbers into decimal numbers:
  1. $1T_{\text{base twelve}}$ 2. $24_{\text{base twelve}}$ 3. $16_{\text{base twelve}}$
  4. $ET_{\text{base twelve}}$ 5. $20_{\text{base twelve}}$ 6. $3T_{\text{base twelve}}$

Change these decimal numbers into base twelve numbers:
  7. 24   8. 13   9. 36
  10. 19   11. 49   12. 170

We can tell the NUMBER of something by looking at it.
The NUMBER can tell us how many, such as how many
    animals are in the parade.
The NUMBER can also tell us the position of something,
    such as the position of each animal in the parade
    from first to last.

To write numbers, we use symbols called NUMERALS.
You have learned that numerals can stand for different
sizes of numbers and that there are many different
numeral systems.

ABOUT THE AUTHOR

David Whitney has written a number of books introducing young readers to the fascinating world of numbers.
His previous books include *The Easy Book of Fractions, The Easy Book of Multiplication, The Easy Book of Division,* and *The Easy Book of Sets.* The author was educated at the University of Kansas and now lives in Chappaqua, New York. He is married and is the father of five children.